On Independence Day

El día de la Independencia

written by Judy Zocchi

illustrated by Rebecca Wallis

dingles&company New Jersey

First printing

PUBLISHED BY dingles&company
P.O. Box 508 • Sea Girt, New Jersey • 08750
WEBSITE: www.dingles.com • E-MAIL: info@dingles.com

Library of Congress Catalog Card No.: 2004091734
ISBN: 1-891997-44-0

Printed in the United States of America

For Marie and Jimmy

ART DIRECTION & DESIGN Barbie Lambert
EDITED BY Andrea Curley
SPANISH EDITED BY John Page
RESEARCH AND ADDITIONAL COPY WRITTEN BY Robert Neal Kanner
EDUCATIONAL CONSULTANT Anita Tarquinio-Marcocci
CRAFT CREATED BY the Aldorasi family
ASSISTANT DESIGNER Erin Collity
PHOTOGRAPHY BY Sara Sagliano
PRE-PRESS BY Pixel Graphics

Holiday Happenings

examines the
most popular holidays
celebrated by various cultures.
The series explains
the origin of each day
as well as popular traditions
and activities
associated with it.

On Independence Day you might decorate your front porch

El día de la Independencia puedes decorar tu patio principal

with red, white, and blue.

de rojo, blanco, y azul.

Then you hang the American flag
for everyone to view.

Luego cuelgas la bandera
Americana para que todos la vean.

It is a custom in the United States to celebrate Independence Day with a parade to honor America's fight for freedom.

On Independence Day you might watch a parade

¡El día de la Independencia puedes mirar un desfile

Es una tradición en los Estados Unidos de celebrar el día de la Independencia con un desfile para honrar la lucha americana por la libertad.

with a drum major and marching band,

con un tambor mayor y una banda musical,

and stand by the curb
waving a flag in your hand!

y estar parado al borde de
la acera agitando una
bandera en tu mano!

On Independence Day you might go to a picnic

El día de la Independencia puedes ir a un picnic

At picnics and barbecues, people usually serve simple food that can be brought and cooked outside. They include hamburgers, hot dogs, potato salad, and soda.

and eat potato salad and a hot dog.

y comer ensalada de patatas y un perro caliente.

En los picnics y en las barbacoas, la gente comúnmente sirve comida sencilla que se puede traer y cocinar afuera. Esta incluye hamburguesas, perros calientes, ensalada de patata, y soda.

Then you play summer games like horseshoes or leap frog!

¡Luego juegas juegos de verano como herraduras o salta rana!

On Independence Day you might climb into the car

El día de la Independencia puedes montarte al auto

with a blanket or a chair,

con una cobija o una silla,

then join your neighbors
to watch fireworks
explode in the air.

luego encontrarte con tus vecinos
para mirar fuegos artificiales
explotar en el aire.

Independence Day is a national holiday in the United States and is celebrated on July 4. It is celebrated each year on the anniversary of the adoption of the Declaration of Independence. In the early 1700s, America consisted of thirteen colonies that were ruled by England. Once England started taxing the colonists and making unfair demands, the colonists became angry. After major fighting broke out between the colonies and England, representatives from the colonies met in 1776 to vote on whether the colonies should break free from England. This was the first Continental Congress. A committee of five men wrote the colonies' "declaration of independence" from England. On July 2, 1776, the Continental Congress voted unanimously in favor of independence. However, the holiday is celebrated on July 4, the day the Declaration of Independence was approved. Americans commemorate the day with picnics, parades, patriotic music, and firework displays.

El día de la Independencia es una fiesta nacional en los Estados Unidos y se celebra el 4 de julio. Se celebra cada año en el aniversario de la adopción de la Declaración de Independencia. En los inicios de 1700s, América consistía de trece colonias que estaban bajo el dominio de Inglaterra. Una vez que Inglaterra comenzó a imponer impuestos a los colonos y hacer demandas injustas, los colonos se enfadaron. Después de que una gran pelea se manifestó entre las colonias e Inglaterra, representantes de las colonias se reunieron en 1776 a someter a votación si las colonias debiesen liberarse de Inglaterra. Esto fue el primer Congreso Continental. Un comité de cinco hombres escribió la "declaración de independencia" de Inglaterra para las colonias. El 2º de julio de 1776, el Congreso Continental votó con unanimidad a favor de la independencia. Sin embargo, el día festivo se celebra el 4 de julio, el día que la Declaración de Independencia se aprobó. Americanos conmemoran el día con picnics, desfiles, música patriota, y despliegues de fuegos artificiales.

DID YOU KNOW...

Use the Holiday Happenings series to expose children to the world around them.

- The original Liberty Bell was cast in London in 1752. It arrived safely at the Philadelphia State House (Independence Hall) but cracked at the first strike of the bell.
- A word is misspelled on the Liberty Bell! "Pennsylvania" is spelled "Pensylvania"!
- John Hancock and Charles Thomson were the only members of the Continental Congress who signed the Declaration of Independence on July 4, 1776. The last signer, Thomas McKean, a representative from Delaware, didn't sign it until 1781!
- People who make fireworks wear only cotton all the way down to their underwear. Static electricity in synthetic clothing can ignite fireworks!

BUILDING CHARACTER...

Use the Holiday Happenings series to help instill positive character traits in your children. This Independence Day emphasize Cooperation.

- What does cooperation mean?
- Do you think it is important to be a good team player? Why or why not?
- Why do you think it was important for the founders of the United States to cooperate while they were building a country?
- Give an example of a situation in your life that required teamwork or cooperation.

CULTURE CONNECTION...

Use the Holiday Happenings series to expand children's view of other cultures.

- Find out which countries have an Independence Day or similar holiday.
- How do they celebrate the holiday?
- Are these celebrations similar to the way you celebrate Independence Day?

TRY SOMETHING NEW...

Encourage your classmates to work as a team the next time you are assigned a group project. Help them to think about what role they can play to help bring about the best result.

For more information on the Holiday Happenings series or to find activities
that coordinate with it, explore our website at **www.dingles.com**.

Craft — Independence Day Food Flags

Goal: To create decorative, patriotic flags to place in such Independence Day barbeque foods as hamburger buns, deviled eggs, and brownies

Craft: Food flags in honor of Independence Day

Materials: a ruler, paper, scissors, glue, toothpicks, crayons and/or markers

Directions:

1. Gather materials.

2. Cut out several 5-inch-x-1½-inch strips of paper.

3. To make each food flag, fold a strip of paper in half. Then put glue in the crease and along the outer edges of the right side of each strip of paper.

4. Place a toothpick in the bottom half of each crease so half of the toothpick extends past the paper strip.

5. Fold each strip in half along the crease to seal the top half of the toothpick inside of the strip.

6. Decorate the food flags with crayons and markers. Use patriotic symbols, for example, the American flag, Uncle Sam, fireworks, and the Liberty Bell.

7. With an adult's permission, place the Independence Day food flags in your barbeque treats!

8. **Important**: Remember to remove the flags before eating the food.

Judy Zocchi

is the author of the Global Adventures, Holiday Happenings, Click & Squeak's Computer Basics, and Paulie and Sasha series. She is a writer and lyricist who holds a bachelor's degree in fine arts/theater from Mount Saint Mary's College and a master's degree in educational theater from New York University. She lives in Manasquan, New Jersey, with her husband, David.

Rebecca Wallis

was born in Cornwall, England, and has a bachelor's degree in illustration from Falmouth College of Arts. She has illustrated a wide variety of books for children, and she divides her time between Cornwall and London.